The Lightning Thief

by
Rick Riordan

Teacher Guide

Written by
Linda Herman

Note

The 2006 Hyperion Paperbacks edition of the novel, © 2005 by Rick Riordan, was used to prepare this guide. The page references may differ in other editions. Novel ISBN: 0-7868-3865-5

Please note: Please assess the appropriateness of this book for the age level and maturity of your students prior to reading and discussing it with them.

ISBN 978-1-56137-718-3

To order, contact your local school supply store, or—

Novel Units, Inc.
P.O. Box 97
Bulverde, TX 78163-0097

Web site: novelunits.com

Table of Contents

Skills and Strategies

Comprehension
Predicting, plot development, cause/effect

Literary Elements
Story mapping, characterization, setting, conflict, theme, point of view, figurative language

Vocabulary
Context clues, definitions, homophones, root words, target words

Listening/Speaking
Discussion, oral presentation, drama

Writing
Creative writing, personal narrative, dialogue, poetry, journalism, myths

Critical Thinking
Brainstorming, research, compare/contrast, analysis, evaluation

Across the Curriculum
Literature—Hero's Journey, Greek mythology, mythical creatures; Social Studies—culture, history, maps and geography, time lines, architecture, family relationships, friendship, bullies, Olympics; Health—nutrition, vegetarianism, phobias; Science—holography, archaeology, echidnas, earthquakes, tides; Math—computation, budgeting; Music—appropriate selections; Art—design, models, illustration

Genre: fantasy, mythology, adventure

Setting: present-day United States

Point of View: first person

Themes: coming of age, individuality, friendship, family, heroism, leadership, responsibility, loyalty, faith, betrayal, learning disabilities, civilization, environmental conservation

Conflict: person vs. self, person vs. person, person vs. society, person vs. nature

Style: narrative

Tone: conversational, humorous

Summary

Twelve-year-old Percy Jackson struggles with dyslexia, attention-deficit hyperactivity disorder (ADHD), and low self-esteem. No matter how hard he tries, he cannot stay out of trouble and must enroll in a new school every year. Then Percy loses his mother in a battle with the Minotaur, and he finds refuge at a nearby farm, Camp Half-Blood, a home for the children of mortals and the Twelve Olympians. There he learns the truth: Greek gods live in the United States, the heart of Western civilization, and he is a son of the Sea God, Poseidon. His learning disabilities are the side effects of his latent demigod powers, and he has been moved from school to school in the interest of his safety. Percy works to develop his abilities and receives a quest, one that the Oracle predicts will be a partial failure and result in betrayal by a friend. Percy must retrieve and return the master lightning bolt stolen from Zeus to prevent a war between the gods. Joined by his satyr friend Grover and Annabeth, a daughter of Athena, Percy makes a harrowing journey to the Underworld, along the way encountering monsters, gods, and a phantom evil force. Percy learns about faith, friendship, and acceptance, and he embraces his destiny as a hero.

About the Author

Born and raised in San Antonio, Texas, Rick Riordan graduated with degrees in English and history from the University of Texas at Austin and received his teaching credentials from the University of Texas at San Antonio. He was a reluctant reader until middle school, when he discovered *The Lord of the Rings* and an English teacher demonstrated how Tolkien's work was based on Norse mythology. Riordan has been reading mythology ever since. He taught in Texas and California for 15 years and incorporated mythology into his curriculum. In 2002, Saint Mary's Hall in San Antonio made him the first recipient of its Master Teacher Award.

Today, Riordan is a full-time writer. He is the author of the Tres Navarre series for adults, winner of the mystery genre's prestigious Shamus, Anthony, and Edgar® awards, and the creator of the new multi-author series, *The 39 Clues*, for which he wrote the first book, the #1 *New York Times* bestselling *The Maze of Bones*. Leaving teaching behind was a difficult decision, yet Riordan says, "I'm still teaching, but as an author, and my 'classroom' has hundreds of thousands of kids in it!" Of writing for kids, he says, "I get the sense that I am making a real impact on their lives. I love it when the Percy Jackson series turns kids into readers."

Riordan's highly acclaimed *Percy Jackson and the Olympians* series is a #1 *New York Times* bestseller. *The Lightning Thief*, the first in the five-book series, won numerous awards. It was the *School Library Journal*'s Best Book of 2005, was chosen as a *New York Times* Notable Book of 2005, and has been made into a 20th Century Fox film. Riordan created Percy Jackson when he ran out of

Greek mythology bedtime stories for his son, a reluctant reader diagnosed with dyslexia and ADHD. He gave the character the same learning disorders as his son to show that "It's not a bad thing to be different. Sometimes, it's the mark of being very, very talented." Through research and experience, Riordan knows that "dyslexic/ADHD kids are creative, 'outside-the-box' thinkers," who can be successful adults if they can get through the tough school years. *The Lightning Thief* is intended to honor these kids and to interest all kids in Greek mythology.

Characters

Perseus "Percy" Jackson: hero; 12-year-old demigod son of Poseidon; believes ADHD is the cause of his day-to-day difficulties

Sally Jackson: Percy's mother; loving and self-sacrificing; attempts to protect Percy by hiding his heritage

"Smelly" Gabe Ugliano: Percy's stepfather; self-centered, abusive, alcoholic poker player; His stench prevents monsters from locating Percy.

Grover Underwood: Percy's best friend; a satyr assigned to guard Percy; dreams of finding Pan

Annabeth Chase: demigoddess daughter of Athena; wants to be an architect; has a Yankees cap with the power of invisibility

Luke: 19-year-old demigod son of Hermes; Percy's friend at Camp Half-Blood

Clarisse: demigod daughter of Ares; leader of the bullies at Camp Half-Blood

Nancy Bobofit: redhead; bully at Yancy Academy

Mr. Brunner/Chiron: Percy's mentor; Latin teacher at Yancy Academy; Chiron, the centaur, at Camp Half-Blood; teacher of heroes for as long as humanity needs him

Mrs. Dodds: Percy's math teacher; one of the three Furies from the Underworld, often referred to as the Kindly Ones

Mr. D: Dionysus, the god of wine; director of Camp Half-Blood

The Oracle: spirit of Delphi, speaker of the prophecies of Phoebus Apollo, slayer of the mighty Python; lives in attic of the Big House at Camp Half-Blood

Argus: head of security at Camp Half-Blood; has eyes covering his body

Aunty Em: Medusa; Percy, Grover, and Annabeth battle her at the beginning of their journey.

Echidna and the Chimera: monsters; Echidna is the Chimera's mother; battle Percy at the Gateway Arch in St. Louis

Crusty: Procrustes, the Stretcher; battles Percy, Grover, and Annabeth in Los Angeles

Charon: ferryman of the dead; fond of drachmas and Italian suits

Ares: god of war; manipulative and egotistical; toys with Percy but is himself a pawn

Hades: god of the Underworld and guard of Tartarus; presumed to have stolen Zeus's master bolt to start a war; His weapon, the helm of darkness, is stolen.

Zeus: king of the gods; god of the sky; Percy's uncle; responsible for unusual weather and is the reason Percy must avoid air travel; His weapon, the master bolt, is stolen.

Poseidon: god of the sea; Percy's father; returned to the sea before Percy's birth, though Percy believes he has a memory of his father's smile

Background Information

The Hero's Journey, also called the Hero's Quest or Monomyth, is a pattern found in mythology as well as today's literature, drama, and movies, and is easily observed in fantasies such as *The Lightning Thief.* It is a useful tool to analyze literature, to teach writing, or to discover more about oneself. The term "Hero's Journey" is credited to Joseph Campbell in *The Hero with a Thousand Faces* (Princeton University Press, 1949). In his study of mythology, Campbell identified common elements of a hero's quest and the archetypes of a hero, the latter based on the psychology of Carl Jung. Another excellent source for further insight is Christopher Vogler's *The Writer's Journey: Mythic Structure for Writers* (Michael Wiese Productions, 1992, 1998, 2007). Sources vary on the number of stages in the Hero's Journey; however, the stages are not meant to be followed as a formula but to be used in various combinations. Christopher Vogler, on page 26 of his 2nd Edition, recaps the Hero's Journey as follows:

1. Heroes are introduced in the ORDINARY WORLD, where
2. they receive the CALL TO ADVENTURE.
3. They are RELUCTANT at first or REFUSE THE CALL, but
4. are encouraged by a MENTOR to
5. CROSS THE FIRST THRESHOLD and enter the Special World, where
6. they encounter TESTS, ALLIES, AND ENEMIES.
7. They APPROACH THE INMOST CAVE, crossing a second threshold
8. where they endure the ORDEAL.
9. They take possession of their REWARD and
10. are pursued on THE ROAD BACK to the Ordinary World.
11. They cross the third threshold, experience a RESURRECTION, and are transformed by the experience.
12. They RETURN WITH THE ELIXIR, a boon or treasure to benefit the Ordinary World.

Initiating Activities

1. Discussion: Tell students that *The Lightning Thief* takes place in the present-day United States. Discuss how modern society might affect the Greek gods (e.g., technology, science). Ask students to brainstorm what American cities and/or landforms could be the locations of Mount Olympus and the Underworld.
2. Comprehension: Display a family tree for the Greek gods and goddesses (available on the Internet). Have students highlight names as they find them in the novel.
3. Research: References to classical mythology and its terminology are commonly used today. They can be found in many English words and phrases (e.g., academy, Midas touch), science (e.g., Echo), anatomy (e.g., Achilles tendon), advertising and brand names (e.g., Hyperion), and pop culture, including movies, literature, and song lyrics. Have students work in teams and locate as many mythological references as possible. Teams should write their findings on colored strips of construction paper and then combine the strips into chains.
4. Art: *The Lightning Thief* references some of the Greek gods' magical weapons and symbols. For example, the main weapon of Zeus, the god of the sky, is a lightning bolt and his symbol

is an eagle. Have students create bookmarks that illustrate what symbols would best suit them. On the back of their bookmarks, students should explain their choices.

5. Literary Analysis: Discuss with students the Hero's Journey (see Background Information on page 5 of this guide). Explain the usefulness of the Hero's Journey in analyzing books, movies, and the real-world journeys every person faces. Have students create reading journals to record Percy's Hero's Journey in *The Lightning Thief*. Students should update their journals after reading each chapter.
6. Prediction: Have students begin the Prediction Chart on page 31 of this guide.

Vocabulary Activities

1. Vocabulary Clues: List vocabulary words on the board. Read clues to the class such as "The word has 'X' number of vowels (or syllables)" and "A synonym (or antonym) for the word is...." Give the word's definition as the final clue. Then call on students to name the vocabulary words.
2. Vocabulary Tic-Tac-Toe: Select nine students to sit in three rows of three in the classroom. Give each student a large cutout of an X and an O. Then select two other students: one student is "X," and the other is "O." Student X is asked to define a vocabulary word. S/he must choose one of the nine students sitting in the square to define the word and then state whether s/he agrees or disagrees with the given definition. If Student X correctly agrees or disagrees with the given definition, the sitting student displays an X. If Student X incorrectly agrees or disagrees, the sitting student displays an O. Alternate turns between Students O and X. The first student to have three Xs or Os in a row (vertical, horizontal, or diagonal) is the winner.
3. Homophones: List the following pairs of homophones on the bulletin board. Instruct students to write a sentence for each word. Their sentences should show the different meanings of each homophone: frieze/freeze, feat/feet, berths/births, queued/cued, and whaling/wailing.
4. Root Word Meanings: Have students find the root word for the following vocabulary words from the novel: kleptomaniac, holographic, propaganda, revelation, illumination, pathetic, reincarnated, and hippodrome. Students should answer the following questions: What is the root word's meaning? What is the meaning of the prefix or suffix added to the word? What is the meaning of the vocabulary word? How has the root word's meaning changed?
5. Target Word Charts: Have students complete Target Word Charts (see page 32 of this guide) of nouns found in the novel. Examples from vocabulary lists include: sphinx, minions, pavilion, abyss, asterisk, portcullis, and summit.

Chapters 1–2

Twelve-year-old Percy Jackson has dyslexia, attention deficit hyperactivity disorder (ADHD), and a talent for causing trouble. However, the events that occur on a school field trip to a museum's Greek and Roman display are unusual even for him, and they result in his expulsion from yet another boarding school. Percy's confusion grows when he overhears his best friend, Grover, and his Latin teacher, Mr. Brunner, worriedly discussing that Percy's life is in peril. On the bus trip home, three old women knitting an enormous pair of socks stare at Percy. When one woman snips the yarn in half, Grover bemoans, "They never get past sixth [grade]" (p. 28).

Vocabulary

expelled
kleptomaniac
sphinx
stele
immortal
scythe
dyslexia
attention deficit disorder
frieze
talons
vaporized
contaminated
squalls
solstice
ignorance

Discussion Questions

1. Why does Percy believe he is a troubled kid? Can you think of another explanation for his problems? *(Percy has attended six different schools in six years and has bad things happen to him on field trips. He has been diagnosed with dyslexia and attention deficit hyperactivity disorder [ADHD], which he has been told causes his brain to misinterpret certain events in his life. Answers will vary, but it is reasonable to say that Percy may have special abilities. He notices things other students do not, such as strange weather and Mrs. Dodds' unnatural movements. Also, it is noteworthy that after Nancy angers Percy, the other kids say that she was "grabbed" by the fountain.)*
2. Why is Mr. Brunner's class the only one that does not bore Percy? What kind of person is Mr. Brunner? *(Mr. Brunner brings history to life and makes learning interesting through the use of stories, jokes, games, and his weapon collection. Answers will vary. Mr. Brunner is a mentor, and he seems to have a special interest in Percy. He only accepts the best from Percy, and this pushes Percy to study harder.)*
3. Mr. Brunner only gives Percy half credit because Percy cannot explain how the myth about the battle between the Titans and the gods applies to real life. How do you think myths apply to real life? *(Answers will vary. Greek mythology's influence is found in modern literature, art, movies, science, athletics, and is the source of many English words. These myths and their concepts, such as heroism, love, and death, are useful tools to analyze modern culture or to better understand oneself. Also, they provide insights into the beliefs and culture of Ancient Greece. The personal importance of Greek mythology to Percy is revealed as the story progresses.)*
4. What do you learn from the battle scene between Percy and Mrs. Dodds? Which piece of information do you think is most important? *(Mrs. Dodds is not working alone, and she knows something about Percy that he does not. Mrs. Dodds is not human, and she intends to harm Percy. Mr. Brunner's sudden and timely arrival implies he also knows things that Percy does not. Mr. Brunner's pen/sword is magical. Answers will vary.)*
5. Why does Percy become "cranky and irritable most of the time" (p. 17)? What is the result of his moodiness? *(Percy is confused because everyone at school insists Mrs. Dodds never existed. Fear of the monster Mrs. Dodds became and threatening weather add to his moodiness. Percy's grades fall, and he causes trouble until he is expelled from Yancy Academy.)*

6. Through eavesdropping, Percy learns that Mr. Brunner and Grover believe he is in danger. What do you think would have happened if Percy had announced his presence? *(Answers will vary. Percy might have learned the truth about Mrs. Dodds, found out what kind of danger he is in, and discovered what others know about him. Discussing his concerns with Mr. Brunner and Grover may have made Percy feel better.)*
7. How does Percy interpret Mr. Brunner's comments about his being expelled? What do you think Mr. Brunner is trying to tell Percy? *(Percy hears his favorite teacher tell him that he does not belong at the school, that he cannot handle it, and that he is not normal. Answers will vary. Mr. Brunner is encouraging Percy, trying to let him know that being expelled is not some indication of failure on Percy's part. He wants Percy to know that it is the school, not Percy, that is inadequate and that things are happening for reasons Percy does not yet understand.)*
8. What comparison does Percy make between himself and the other kids at school? What does this tell you about him? *(All of the students are juvenile delinquents, but because the other kids have rich and famous fathers, Percy feels like "a nobody, from a family of nobodies" [p. 22]. Answers will vary. Percy has low self-esteem. He wants to feel important and may be jealous of his classmates.)*
9. What is the significance of the old woman cutting the yarn? Predict who the three old women are. *(Someone is going to die. Answers will vary, but students familiar with Greek mythology will recognize the women as the Three Fates; the yarn represents someone's life thread.)*
10. **Prediction:** Who is Grover talking about when he says, "Always sixth grade. They never get past sixth" (p. 28)?

Supplementary Activities

1. Literary Analysis: Reread page 1 of the novel. Write a paragraph that evaluates the effectiveness of opening the story with a warning to readers.
2. Research/Speaking: Research attention deficit hyperactivity disorder. Lead a classroom discussion about whether Percy's actions are consistent with ADHD symptoms such as inattentiveness, impulsiveness, and hyperactivity.
3. Greek Mythology: Working in teams, begin an illustrated encyclopedia of Greek mythology. Include entries for the gods and goddesses, creatures and monsters, and myths found in the novel. "The Battle of the Gods and Titans" (see Chapter 1) will be your first entry. Use reference materials to complete each entry.

Chapters 3–4

Percy and his mother leave Smelly Gabe at home to vacation at their cabin on the beach in Montauk. There they discuss Percy's father, who never returned from a sea voyage. In the middle of the night, during a freak hurricane, Grover pounds on the door, shouting that something is behind him. As they race for the car, Percy realizes Grover is not wearing pants and that he has shaggy hindquarters and cloven hooves. Percy's mother admits she has been selfish keeping Percy near her instead of sending him to the safety of the summer camp Percy's father recommended. They flee in Gabe's Camaro, and Grover is injured when the car is struck by lightning and swerves into a ditch. At the camp's border, the Minotaur from Greek mythology attacks Percy's mother and she vanishes in a flash of golden light. With newfound strength, Percy slays the Minotaur. He then carries Grover to the camp's farmhouse before collapsing.

Vocabulary

terminal
novelist
reeked
rebellious
hyperactive
resented
goading
artillery
mallets
cloven
lanolin
minions
chassis
dissolved
holographic

Discussion Questions

1. What kind of person is Sally Jackson? Why might she have married Gabe Ugliano, especially since he smells and does not treat her well? *(Percy says his mother is the nicest lady in the world and that she deserves a better life. Despite hardships and broken dreams, Sally Jackson remains upbeat and sees the good in others. She is a kind person who makes sacrifices to support and keep peace in her family. Answers will vary.)*
2. What does Gabe's behavior tell you about him? *(Answers will vary, but students should infer that Gabe is self-centered and abusive. He cares about his own comfort and things like his car more than his wife and stepson.)*
3. What is the importance of blue food? *(Percy's mother goes out of her way to serve blue food because Gabe once said there was no such thing. The food, along with keeping her maiden name, is how Percy's mother shows her rebellious streak and stands up to Gabe.)*
4. What does Percy know about his father? How does he feel about his father? *(Percy's parents were only together one summer at Montauk beach, yet his mother still cares for his father. Percy shares his father's black hair and green eyes. Percy's father is powerful, yet gentle, and he left on an important journey across the Atlantic from which he never returned. Percy's father has never seen him, yet Percy remembers him. Percy is angry at and resents his father for leaving his mother in a situation that resulted in her marrying Gabe. Percy believes his father did not have the guts to marry his mother.)*
5. How is Percy's conversation with his mother about leaving Yancy Academy similar to the conversation he had with Mr. Brunner? How is it different? *(Answers will vary. Both adults want to keep Percy safe and attempt to encourage him, but both are obviously keeping secrets. Percy misunderstands both adults, thinking he is unwanted because he is not normal. With Mr. Brunner, Percy is embarrassed in front of the class and walks away hurt before Mr. Brunner can articulate what he means to say. With his mother, Percy is hurt that she wants to send him away again but learns that she does it to keep him safe. Percy also discovers his mother has not sent him to the summer camp recommended by his father because she fears she might never see him again.)*
6. What can you predict from the information revealed in Percy's dream? *(Answers will vary. A white horse and a golden eagle are battling each other while an evil voice encourages the violence. Those familiar with mythology may associate the eagle with Zeus and the horse with Poseidon. The dream may mean that Zeus and Poseidon are being manipulated into attacking each other by an evil force. That Percy feels he must end the violence suggests that he may soon become responsible for helping Zeus and Poseidon make peace.)*
7. What does Grover say was the purpose of the Mist? Why didn't this work? *(The Mist was supposed to make Percy think the Kindly One was a hallucination. Instead Percy started realizing who he is.)*
8. Percy's mother says, "I've been worried about an attack for a long time. I should have expected this. I was selfish, keeping you near me" (p. 51). Do you think Percy's mother is selfish or brave? *(Answers will vary. Keeping Percy near her may put him in danger, but it is only natural that a mother would want to keep her young son relatively close to her. Percy's mother is a loving and positive influence in Percy's life, and she does her best to keep him safe, finding different schools for him to attend each year. When they are attacked, she willingly sacrifices herself to protect Percy.)*

9. During the fight with the Minotaur, which of Percy's actions are heroic? *(Percy refuses to leave his mother and Grover in danger, overcomes his fear and instinct to bolt, thinks quickly under enormous pressure, and ignores his own needs until Grover is safe.)*
10. **Prediction:** Will Percy and Grover be safe at the camp? Explain your answer.

Supplementary Activities

1. Critical Thinking: Research factors that influence people to become bullies. Create a profile of Smelly Gabe. Explain why Gabe acts the way he does based on information from your profile.
2. Geography: Locate Montauk on a map of New York, and browse through a travel guide about the location. Discuss why Percy's mother and father chose to vacation there.
3. Health: Research news stories and science articles about blue food and blue food coloring. Answer these questions: What foods are naturally blue? Why is blue food considered unappetizing? Does food coloring cause hyperactivity in kids?
4. Art: Build a model labyrinth in which to keep the Minotaur. Be creative in your choice of material (e.g., clay, sugar cubes).

Chapters 5–6

Grover, Annabeth, and a "surfer dude" covered with eyes nurse Percy back to health. He meets the camp director, Mr. D (Dionysus, god of wine), and discovers that Mr. Brunner is really Chiron the centaur, trainer of heroes. Chiron explains that the Greek gods live in America, the epicenter of Western civilization. As Percy tours the campgrounds, he learns the camp is a training ground for children of the gods, and that he too is a half-blood, though which god is his father has yet to be determined. When Clarisse, a daughter of Ares, and her friends drag Percy into the girls' bathroom for a mean-spirited initiation ceremony, Percy reacts and the plumbing explodes, dousing the girls into submission.

Vocabulary
recoiled pavilion archery pinochle feat endeavors primitive incinerates facades hewn humanity caduceus archetypes ambrosia initiation

Discussion Questions

1. How is Mr. D similar to Smelly Gabe? Why might gods in myths have the same traits as humans? *(Mr. D doesn't dress well, drinks, and plays cards. He is outspoken and rude. Answers will vary. Discussion could cover how shared traits allow people to better relate to the gods, which makes it easier to understand the myths' messages.)*
2. Mr. D and Chiron disagree with Percy about gods being "what people believed before there was science" (p. 68). Can science disprove the gods' existence? *(Answers will vary. Science provides some explanations for natural phenomena. However, science does not explain all known phenomena, and its explanations have changed as technology has advanced. To date, science has not disproved the existence of the gods.)*
3. Why did Mount Olympus move from Greece? Which country do you think Olympus will move to after the United States? *(The gods and Western civilization are inextricably tied. Greece was once the epicenter of social progress in the West. As the epicenter of Western social progress changed, so too did the gods' base of operations. Answers will vary.)*

4. Why might Dionysus and the Council of Cloven Elders believe Grover failed his assignment as Percy's keeper? What points should Grover make on his own behalf? *(Grover loses Percy in New York, is unable to save Percy's mother, and has to be carried by Percy to Camp Half-Blood. However, Grover shows courage by never intentionally abandoning Percy. Despite the fact that Percy ditches him at the bus terminal, Grover manages to arrive at the beach cabin ahead of the Minotaur, allowing Percy time to escape and eventually reach the camp.)*
5. Why does Percy ask Chiron whether the Underworld is real? *(Answers will vary, but students should infer that Percy is wondering what has happened to his mother and if she can still be rescued.)*
6. Chiron says he has gained much and given up much from being "a teacher of heroes as long as humanity needed [him]," and that the work is "horribly depressing, at times, but never boring" (p. 82). What do you think Chiron means? *(Answers will vary. Chiron has the satisfaction of seeing his students accomplish amazing things from his teachings as well as the progress of mankind over the centuries. However, he has most likely seen terrible things happen to his students [since heroes' work is dangerous and often requires high-stakes decision-making] as well as many historic tragedies.)*
7. Why is Percy assigned to Cabin Eleven? *(Campers are assigned cabins based on the identity of their parents. Until Percy's father's identity is known, Percy, like all newcomers and visitors, will stay in Cabin Eleven because it belongs to Hermes, the god of travelers.)*
8. What do you think Clarisse means when she says, "Like [Percy is] 'Big Three' material"? *(Answers will vary. "Big Three" refers to the most powerful gods—Zeus, Poseidon, and Hades. Clarisse is sarcastically dismissing Percy, but if Percy is "'Big Three' material," it means that one of those gods is his father.)*
9. Do you think the incident with Clarisse in the bathroom will affect how other campers view Percy? *(Answers will vary. Annabeth now wants Percy on her team for capture the flag. Clarisse's friends may become Percy's enemies. Most campers are aware of Percy's battle with the Minotaur and know that he is powerful, but the bathroom incident may make them wonder more about whom his father is.)*
10. **Prediction:** Which god is Percy's father? Why do you think so?

Supplementary Activities

1. Comprehension: Create an orientation film to welcome new members to Camp Half-Blood.
2. Critical Thinking: Percy thinks myths are "what people believed before there was science" (p. 68). Write a myth to explain a natural phenomenon.
3. Social Studies: Write a brief report that describes the three types of columns used in Greek architecture (Doric, Ionic, and Corinthian). Illustrate your report with examples of each column type as found on buildings in the United States.
4. Literary Analysis: Begin Character Webs (see page 33 of this guide) for Grover, Annabeth, and Luke. Add information as you read the story.

Chapters 7–8

Luke befriends Percy and helps him train. Annabeth says there will be trouble if something stolen at the gods' annual council is not returned by the summer solstice. Grover explains that although Zeus, Poseidon, and Hades agreed not to sire any more heroes, promises have been broken. At the camp's capture-the-flag contest, Clarisse and her teammates attack Percy, but he fights them off and his wounds heal when he steps into a creek. With the entire camp watching, a hellhound, which could only be summoned by someone in camp, attacks Percy. Again, he enters the water to heal. A sign of acknowledgment from his father appears, the green trident of Poseidon.

Vocabulary

oracle
quest
prophecy
omen
conch
brazier
laurels
sparring
manic
prominently
maiming
ally
elated
cascade
trident

Discussion Questions

1. Why do you think Percy is reluctant to admit that his father is a god? *(Answers will vary. Accepting that his father is a god will force Percy to seriously redefine who he is and take on many responsibilities. Also, if Percy's father is a god, his father is not lost or dead and has always had the means to contact him and his mother.)*
2. Annabeth's mother is Athena, the goddess of wisdom and battle. Does Annabeth share these traits with her mother? *(Answers will vary. Annabeth's explanations about gods and camp demonstrate intelligence. She realizes early on that Percy will make a valuable addition to her capture-the-flag team, and the strategy she devises to defeat Clarisse's team is clever. Also, Athena and Poseidon are rivals, and Annabeth is at times rude to or inconsiderate of Percy for seemingly no reason.)*
3. Why does Percy compare the gods' treatment of their children to rich parents' treatment of their kids at Yancy Academy? Is it reasonable for Percy to expect gods to behave better? *(Gods and rich parents are often too "busy" to pay attention to their children. Sending demigods to Camp Half-Blood is similar to rich parents sending their children to boarding schools in that the children are cared for but are not inconveniencing their parents. Answers will vary. Discussion should cover whether the superiority of the gods gives them the right to put their godly responsibilities first or whether they should be better examples as parents and more aware of their children's feelings of abandonment.)*
4. Why isn't Chiron assigning quests to the demigods? How is Percy important to Annabeth's desire to go on a quest? *(The last quest, Luke's trip to the Garden of the Hesperides, did not go well. Because Chiron said Annabeth is not destined to go on a quest until somebody special arrives at camp, Annabeth hopes Percy is the special person because she desperately wants an opportunity to get out into the world.)*
5. What do Percy's actions at dinner tell you about his thoughts? *(Percy is thinking of his mother and father. He drinks a toast to his mother, and while making a burnt offering, Percy mentally pleads for his father to identify himself.)*
6. What gives Percy renewed strength during sword fighting? How does Luke react? *(Pouring ice water over his head renews his strength. Luke takes a new interest in Percy and presses him harder as if he has found a worthy opponent.)*
7. How does the story of Thalia make Percy feel? Do you think he should feel this way? *(Percy feels "hollow and guilty." He is convinced that he was not as brave as Thalia and that if he had been he might have been able to save his mother. Answers will vary, but it seems that Percy did all he could. He fought the Minotaur with great physical and mental strength without any knowledge of his ancestry or training. Thalia may have known that she was Zeus's daughter and had special powers.)*

8. Annabeth expresses concern upon finding out that Poseidon is Percy's father. Why might she be worried? *(Answers will vary. Annabeth is probably worried because the sign from Poseidon confirms that Poseidon broke the pact he made with Zeus and Hades. Annabeth is most likely thinking of Thalia and her untimely death. Combined with the hellhound attack, the sign from Poseidon makes her realize that Percy and anyone near him [at this point, the whole camp] is in grave danger. She may also be thinking that since Percy is obviously "special," he is the one with whom she will be going on her quest. Athena and Poseidon have an existing rivalry, and she may be concerned that her personality will clash with Percy's.)*
9. **Prediction:** Who do you think summoned the hellhound? What quest will be offered to Percy?

Supplementary Activities

1. Comprehension: Write a eulogy for Thalia.
2. Comprehension: Create a camp newsletter. Write an article that reports on the capture-the-flag competition, the hellhound attack, and Poseidon's acknowledgment of Percy as his son. Report opinions on these events in a "Letters to the Editor" section. Include letters from campers, counselors, and the director, Mr. D.
3. Science: Research holography, and discuss the uses of holograms (e.g., medical devices, credit cards). Then create a scratch hologram (instructions available on the Internet).

Chapters 9–10

Chiron offers Percy a quest that, if successful, will prevent a full-fledged war between the gods. Though Chiron believes Hades is the thief, Zeus has accused Poseidon of having Percy steal his master lightning bolt; Poseidon denies the theft and demands an apology. Percy's quest is to travel to the Underworld, where he will confront Hades and then return Zeus's powerful weapon before the gods' deadline, the summer solstice, which is only ten days away. Percy resents that the father who has ignored him for 12 years suddenly needs him, but he accepts the quest as a way to rescue his mother. Accompanied by Grover and Annabeth, Percy leaves Camp Half-Blood armed with Annabeth's invisibility Yankees cap, Poseidon's magical pen/sword, and a pair of winged shoes given to him by Luke. On the bus out of New York, Mrs. Dodds and the other two Furies attack. Percy vanquishes two before the bus is struck by lightning and explodes. Their food, money, and extra clothes are lost in the blaze, but Percy and his friends escape into a nearby forest.

Discussion Questions

1. Compare and contrast Percy's dream with Chiron's explanation of actual events. *(In Percy's dream, two men in Greek tunics [one blue and one green] fight over a missing object while lightning flashes and waves crash on the beach. This implies a struggle between Zeus and Poseidon. The evil, laughing voice from underground seems to belong to Hades, and the setting is a city by the beach. Chiron confirms the identities of the gods and names Zeus's master lightning bolt as the stolen object. Chiron theorizes that Hades is the only one who would stand to gain from a war between gods and explains that the entrance to the Underworld is in Los Angeles. Chiron's explanation provides details not found in the dream, such as Zeus's accusations and the motives of Zeus, Poseidon, and Hades.)*
2. Which part of the Oracle's prophecy do you think bothers Percy most? Which would most bother you? *(Percy worries about which friend will betray him, especially since he does not have many friends. However, he seems more upset about being sent on a quest that he will fail. Answers will vary. Discussion could cover the importance of friendship versus success.)*

Vocabulary
grappled kowtow arsenal paranoid proverbial prevail tendrils drachmas hyperventilating riveted divine propaganda melancholy careened eternal

3. Why does Chiron believe Hades stole Zeus's master bolt? *(Hades's kingdom would grow more powerful with millions of deaths from a war over the master bolt, and he must hate his brothers for breaking the oath they have forced him to keep. A Fury and a hellhound, both minions of Hades, have come after Percy, the secret son of Poseidon who could help clear his father's name.)*
4. Why does Percy feel anticipation rather than fear about a quest to the Underworld? *(Percy hopes to rescue his mother. He also wants revenge against Hades for taking his mother and sending three monsters after him. Though Percy has mixed emotions about his father, he hates that Hades framed him and his father for stealing the master bolt.)*
5. How are the magical items that Percy and his friends take on the quest associated with the gods? Which item do you think will be the most useful? Why? *(Annabeth's Yankees cap was a birthday present from Athena. Luke's basketball shoes were a gift from Hermes. Percy's pen/sword was a gift from Poseidon. Answers will vary. Discussion should cover the advantages and disadvantages of each magical item's special properties: The cap's wearer becomes invisible; the shoes' wearer can fly [though Percy should not]; the sword has special power, cannot be lost, and will not harm mortals. All three items generate Mist to distort humans' perception of divine or monster-related events.)*
6. Why does Percy ask Chiron about the time before the gods? Do you think Chiron's answer reassures him? *(Percy wants to know whether the gods and humanity will survive if he fails his quest. Answers will vary. He is not reassured when Chiron says that no one knows how long the Age of the West will last and implies that the gods are vulnerable to the same kind of fall the Titans suffered. However, it may be reassuring to know that all he can do is fulfill his destiny.)*
7. Should Percy tell Grover and Annabeth the truth about why he accepted the quest? *(Answers will vary. Not being honest with his friends makes Percy feel guilty and is not a good way to build trust. Grover probably knows the truth because he can read Percy's emotions.)*
8. Based on the battle with the Furies, do you think Percy, Grover, and Annabeth make a good team? Why? *(Answers will vary, but students should infer that the trio works well together as shown by their surviving an attack by the Underworld's three worst monsters. Each person shows quick thinking, bravery, and the willingness to risk his/her life to protect his/her friends.)*
9. **Prediction:** Which friend will betray Percy? How?

Supplementary Activities

1. Compare/Contrast: Create an illustration of the two men fighting on the beach in Percy's dream. Compare and contrast your illustration with those of your classmates. Discuss whether similarities come from details provided in the novel and whether differences come from details filled in by readers' imaginations.
2. Research: Research the Greek Trojan Horse myth. Then research harmful computer programs called Trojan Horses. Write a well-developed paragraph that explains why these programs are named after the Greek myth.
3. Science/Speaking: As Percy does in the book, the people of Ancient Greece consulted the Oracle of Delphi for advice. Find a current, science-based news story about why scientists think natural gas may have played a role in the Oracle's prophecies. Share your findings in class.

4. Personal Narrative: Chiron tells Percy, "Remarkable, really, the lengths to which humans will go to fit things into their version of reality" (p. 155). Write about a time when you misinterpreted something so it would make sense to you.

Chapters 11–12

Percy, Annabeth, and Grover battle Medusa at Aunty Em's Garden Gnome Emporium, a shop full of strange statues. Grover and Annabeth distract Medusa while Percy cuts off her head, which he impertinently sends to Mount Olympus. Camping in a litter-strewn spot in the woods, Grover bemoans the pollution made by humans and tells Percy of his dreams to be the searcher who finds Pan, the god of Wild Places. Grover remarks that the Furies on the bus seemed to be looking for an object, not just Percy. The next morning, Grover meets a lost poodle for whom there is a reward. The poodle agrees to be returned to his family so that Grover, Percy, and Annabeth can afford train tickets.

Vocabulary
braying curio emporium kelp writhing pawn distortion crooned petrify nostalgic despair compelled abyss void treacherous

Discussion Questions

1. In which order do Percy, Grover, and Annabeth sense something is wrong at Aunty Em's Garden Gnome Emporium? Which clues do they notice? When did you know Aunty Em is really Medusa? *(Grover is immediately suspicious about the Emporium, especially after he sees a statue that looks like his Uncle Ferdinand and he smells monsters. Annabeth eventually realizes who Aunty Em is when she hears the story about Medusa and her two sisters. Percy's hunger causes him to ignore his friends' warnings and any suspicions he might have about Aunty Em's veiled head and the fact that she locks the door, does not eat with them, knows Annabeth's name without being told, and seems fascinated with Annabeth's gray eyes. Answers will vary.)*
2. Medusa believes becoming a statue would be less painful for Percy than going to the Underworld. Do you agree or disagree with her? How much should the threat of pain influence someone's decisions? *(Answers will vary, but it is reasonable to say there are serious responsibilities that demand that concerns about personal comfort be put aside for a greater good or purpose.)*
3. Why does Percy send Medusa's head to Mount Olympus? What message is he sending to the gods? *(Percy is angry at the gods for making this quest necessary and for putting obstacles like the weather and the monsters in their way on their first day. Answers will vary, but Percy wants the Olympians to know that he is not their pawn and that he resents being used. He also wants the gods to know that he and his friends are worthy opponents and that they will not be intimidated into abandoning their quest.)*
4. What does Grover mean when he says, "This is a terrible time to be a satyr" (p. 189)? What event would make it a good time to be a satyr? *(Satyrs despair over the pollution of the earth, which began upon the disappearance of Pan, the god of Wild Places. According to Grover, if the satyrs can find Pan, then the god will restore the environment to its natural state and protect his creatures.)*
5. Why does Percy think his quest sounds as hopeless as Grover's dream? Which do you think is more hopeless? *(In 2,000 years, no searcher has ever returned from pursuing Pan. Percy realizes he may not return from the Underworld. Answers will vary.)*

6. The Furies are searching for an object. What does Percy think is odd about this? What object might the Furies be searching for? *(Percy wonders what they would be searching for since they should know that the master bolt is in the Underworld. Answers will vary, but it is possible that the bolt or something belonging to Hades has been lost.)*
7. What does Grover say is the reason Percy sent Medusa's head to Mount Olympus? Does Percy's response sound believable? *(According to Grover, Percy is happy Poseidon claimed him and Percy wants to make Poseidon proud. Sending the head to Olympus ensures that Poseidon notices what Percy has accomplished. Answers will vary, but students should infer that Percy's response sounds defensive.)*
8. In Percy's dream, what does the evil being in the pit want from Percy? What does it offer in return? *(The being wants the master bolt and wants Percy to help it rise from the pit. It offers Percy's mother in return for Percy's help.)*
9. **Prediction:** What will the gods do with Medusa's head?

Supplementary Activities

1. Health: Grover is a vegetarian. Design a brochure that covers the advantages and disadvantages of kids being vegetarian. Be sure to provide answers to questions that someone considering becoming a vegetarian might have.
2. Greek Mythology: Research Percy's namesake. Then compare and contrast Percy and Perseus by completing the graphic organizer on page 34 of this guide.
3. Creative Writing: Create a poem about one of Medusa's statues. You may write your poem from the viewpoint of a viewer or the statue.
4. Comprehension: Imagine that Grover has found Pan. Write a dialogue between Grover and the god of Wild Places discussing environmental concerns.

Chapters 13–14

On the train west, Percy and Annabeth discuss his dream about the thing in the pit and her mortal family, who never wanted her. Percy, Annabeth, and Grover visit the Gateway Arch in St. Louis. At the top of the Arch, Percy loses a battle with the Chimera, the son of Echidna. Percy survives jumping into the Mississippi River and discovers he can breathe underwater. A messenger from Poseidon tells Percy that he must go to the beach in Santa Monica before entering the Underworld. On the riverbank, the media reports that Percy Jackson is a fugitive suspected of multiple crimes.

Discussion Questions

1. Compare Percy's and Annabeth's relationships with their mortal parents. Who do you think has the better home life? *(Percy has to deal with an abusive stepfather, but his mother loved him and wanted him with her. Annabeth's family resents her and wanted her to leave. Answers will vary.)*
2. Why is Annabeth hesitant to cooperate with Percy? Do you think she and Percy will be able to work together? Why? *(Annabeth allows the rivalry between Athena and Poseidon to influence her relationship with Percy. Answers will vary. Annabeth and Percy have already demonstrated that they can work together in battles against the Furies and Medusa. That Athena and Poseidon cooperated to complete the chariot provides Annabeth with a new outlook, which may allow her to cooperate better with Percy.)*

Vocabulary

berths
barter
deceitful
Parthenon
monument
helm
rhinestone
structural
revelation
mortality
embedded
sonar
immune
adolescent
trundled

3. How is Hades's helm of darkness more powerful than Annabeth's Yankees cap? *(The helm does not just make Hades invisible but allows him to become darkness, to move about without being touched, seen, or heard and pass through walls. It also allows him to induce intense fear in others.)*
4. What do Percy's thoughts prior to jumping in the river tell you about him? *(Answers will vary. That Percy worries about the fate of the humans, even as poison courses through his own veins, is heroic. Percy is conflicted about what course of action to take. He thinks of his father's smile and thinks that his father must care about him, but he also reasons that the Mississippi is not "the sea" and hence not the domain of the Sea God. In the end, he comes to view the dive into the river as his best chance for survival [and making the monsters disappear], and his last act before jumping is a prayer to his father, thereby disproving Echidna's accusation that he is "faithless." Percy's leap from the Arch is not one of despair but of faith [however little he may have], not only in his father but in himself and his identity as a son of Poseidon.)*
5. Percy does not feel like a hero, yet the water spirit calls him "brave one" and says, "Your father believes in you" (p. 214). How do you explain this difference of opinion? *(Answers will vary. Percy feels inadequate and thinks that a hero must defeat each monster, not just survive an attack. However, others, including Poseidon, are impressed by the way Percy faces danger even when he is afraid. Ironically, most heroes do not consider themselves heroic.)*
6. The water spirit warns Percy, "...do not trust the gifts" (p. 215). What gifts has Percy received so far? *(Percy has received the flying shoes from Luke and the pen/sword from Chiron/Poseidon.)*
7. The mother of the little boy in the Arch tells the paramedic the truth about the monster, and she recognizes Percy. Why doesn't the paramedic believe her? What does the woman say happened after Percy jumped off the Arch? *(The paramedic thinks medication is affecting the woman, causing her to talk deliriously about monsters. She says the monster disappeared after Percy jumped off the Arch.)*
8. What is the media reporting about Percy? *(The media reports that he may have caused the explosion on the Arch and that he is wanted for the New Jersey bus accident.)*
9. **Prediction:** What will Percy discover in Santa Monica?

Supplementary Activities

1. Geography/History/Math: Use the clues given in the novel and Amtrak and Greyhound schedules (available on the Internet) to map the route of Percy's quest. For each stop along the route, include a brief report about the town. Report on something the town is known for or an interesting fact about its history. Finally, compute how many miles Percy travels.
2. Comprehension: Athena told Annabeth's father that "...heroes [have] to be raised by their mortal parent" (p. 200). Divide a sheet of paper into two columns. In the left column, list possible effects of being raised by a mortal parent. In the right column, list possible effects of being raised by a divine parent. Write a paragraph that explains which parent you think should raise a hero and why.

3. History: Prepare a time line of the Parthenon. Include visual displays and brief reports highlighting important events from its construction to today's restoration project.
4. Science: Create a display about the echidna, the egg-laying mammal named for Echidna, the Mother of Monsters. Include written information and illustrations.

Chapters 15–16

Grover, Percy, and Annabeth contact the camp using a spray gun at a carwash and update Luke on their adventures. Ares, the god of war, offers to help Percy reach Los Angeles and provide information about Sally's fate in exchange for retrieving his shield from an abandoned water park. Percy, Annabeth, and Grover barely escape a trap at the park that Hephaestus had meant for Aphrodite and Ares. True to his word, Ares secures a ride for Percy and his friends in a truck carrying abused zoo animals and reveals that Percy's mother is not dead. Percy learns that Grover's failed mission involved Thalia [Zeus's daughter], Annabeth, and Luke. In Las Vegas, Percy and his friends release the zoo animals. They visit the Lotus Hotel and Casino, where they lose track of time until only one day remains to complete their quest.

Vocabulary
hypnotized proposition marooned asterisk illumination scuttling capsizing barricade humane hostages pathetic mildewed trireme dais sanctuary

Discussion Questions

1. Why are the campers choosing sides? Explain how you think the campers got this information. *(The campers are choosing sides according to their parents' alliances with either Zeus or Poseidon. Someone must have leaked information about the argument between Zeus and Poseidon. Answers will vary.)*
2. Do you think Percy should have told Luke everything about what has happened, including his dreams? Why? *(Answers will vary. Percy does not have enough money to call back and trusts Luke to relay information to Chiron. However, Chiron may not want anyone else to know the details of Percy's quest.)*
3. Why isn't Percy afraid of Ares? *(Ares reminds Percy of other bullies he has faced, and he notices something false in Ares's threatening look, as if the god is nervous. Also Percy's impertinent attitude toward the gods, which is only exacerbated by Ares's presence, is far greater than any fears he has.)*
4. What does Ares mean when he says, "I love this country. Best place since Sparta" (p. 227)? *(Answers will vary. Sparta, a city-state in ancient Greece, had the best trained military of its time and a reputation for being warlike. Ares is saying America is similar in this way. Discussion could cover whether students agree or disagree with Ares based on current news stories about conflicts with other countries and crime rates.)*
5. Annabeth says Ares needs help retrieving his shield because the problem may require brains and Ares only has strength. How do Percy and Annabeth use their brains at the amusement park? *(Percy thinks of using water to escape. Annabeth uses knowledge of physics to safely exit the crashing boat. Her historical knowledge provides insight into Hephaestus's motives.)*
6. Grover does not like being underground. Percy is not comfortable in confined spaces, and Annabeth is afraid of spiders. How does each character deal with his/her phobia? *(Percy and Grover acknowledge their fears and are able to control them. For example, Grover toured the*

underground museum, and Percy rode the elevator at the Arch. Annabeth knows why she has a fear of spiders, but she cannot control her reaction. On the water ride, she freezes and Percy has to help her.)

7. Grover regrets not telling Percy the truth about escorting Thalia to Camp Half-Blood. He says, "I thought if you knew what a failure I was, you wouldn't want me along" (p. 248). Do you think Percy would have asked Grover to join the quest if he had known the truth? Why? *(Answers will vary, but it is reasonable to say that Percy would still want Grover with him. He needs help on the quest, and Grover is his best friend. Furthermore, Percy does not agree with the Council of Cloven Elders about Thalia's death being Grover's fault. He admires Grover for not leaving Annabeth and Luke and respects Grover's talent for finding important half-bloods. Percy believes Grover is a natural searcher, the one who will find Pan.)*
8. What do Percy's, Grover's, and Annabeth's choices of entertainment at the Lotus Casino tell you about them? *(Percy is hyperactive, adventurous, and a thrill seeker as shown by his choice of activities, such as bungee-jumping, virtual-reality laser tag, and FBI sharpshooter, snowboarding, and skiing simulations. Grover eats potato chips to satisfy his voracious goat appetite and plays reverse hunter games that help him vent his frustration with humans' treatment of the natural world. Annabeth, who watches educational TV, plays trivia games, and designs a city on a 3-D game, is curious, intelligent, and creative.)*
9. What does the Lotus Casino represent, and why does the author include this scene? Would you like to spend time at the casino? *(The casino represents the danger of becoming so obsessed with one's own pleasures that one ignores everything else in life. The Lotus Casino is an allusion to the episode in* The Odyssey *where some of Odysseus's men lose all motivation to complete their journey after eating lotus fruit. The author means to make the point that forgetting one's cares may be appealing, but everyone has responsibilities and shirking them indefinitely, at best, leaves one's life empty and meaningless. At worst, living selfishly and irresponsibly harms not only oneself but many other people [as nearly happens in the situation with Percy, Annabeth, and Grover]. This point is particularly important because Percy, Grover, and Annabeth are not just making a literal journey across the country; they are also on a coming-of-age journey, and part of coming of age is accepting and fulfilling one's responsibilities. Answers will vary.)*
10. **Prediction:** Who is the familiar voice in Percy's most recent dream?

Supplementary Activities

1. Health: A phobia is an irrational fear that negatively affects a person's life. Some, like Annabeth's arachnophobia, or fear of spiders, are well known. Zeusophobia, or a fear of God or gods, is a lesser-known phobia. With your teacher's permission, research phobias on the Internet. Answer these questions: Do you think everyone has phobias? Which phobia do you think would be easiest to live with? Which would be the most difficult?
2. Critical Thinking: Each bead on Annabeth's necklace represents the most important event of a particular year at Camp Half-Blood. List the most important events of the last five years in your life, and explain your choices.
3. Creative Writing: Write a story about the summer a centaur wore a prom dress at Camp Half-Blood. Use details from the novel in your story.
4. Critical Thinking: Percy drags Grover and Annabeth from the Lotus Casino with only one day left to complete their quest. Write a paragraph about what they might have seen outside of the casino if they had stayed another month, year, or ten years.

Chapters 17–18

Percy has trouble recalling certain details of his last dream due to his time in the Lotus Casino. Annabeth is concerned about the monster in Percy's dreams but insists that it must be Hades. At the beach in Santa Monica, Percy receives three magical pearls from the same woman who appeared to him in the Mississippi, a Nereid, who tells him he must do what his heart tells him or lose everything. Percy rescues Annabeth and Grover from a water bed salesman, Procrustes, the Stretcher. At the water bed store, Percy finds the address for the entrance to the Underworld. They cross the polluted River Styx after bribing Charon, the ferryman for the dead. Mingling among the dead, Percy and Annabeth play fetch with Cerberus, the three-headed guard dog, to gain entrance into the Underworld.

Vocabulary
infinity hurtling morale shoals sustain brink realm fugitive imperfect spheres confront warbled portcullis queued keening

Discussion Questions

1. What can you determine from Annabeth's reactions to Percy's dream? *(Answers will vary, but students should infer that Annabeth suspects someone other than Hades and is frightened.)*
2. What do you think the Nereid means when she tells Percy, "You have gifts you have only begun to know" (p. 272)? What are Percy's gifts? *(Answers will vary. Though Percy is inexperienced as a hero, he is doing well on his quest. By telling Percy to listen to his heart, the Nereid implies that Percy has wisdom and a strong moral compass. Percy cares for others, has earned the loyalty of his friends, has shown great courage, and is beginning to realize the full extent of his water-based powers.)*
3. The differences between New York and Los Angeles scare Percy. Los Angeles reminds him of Ares. How do you think someone from Los Angeles would describe New York? Which god would you associate with New York? *(Answers will vary. Discussion could cover familiar versus unfamiliar situations, first impressions, and the ways in which cities are different. As the largest city in the United States and the financial center of the world, New York could be associated with Zeus.)*
4. How does Percy get the idea to trick Crusty? *(Answers will vary. Suggestions: Percy remembers the story of Procrustes; therefore, he recalls that Theseus tricked Procrustes into getting fitted to his famous bed. Percy turns Crusty's "excess[ive] hospitality" against him.)*
5. What do you think the "DOA" of DOA Recording Studios stands for? *(Answers will vary, but students should infer that DOA stands for "dead on arrival" as the studio is the entrance to the Underworld.)*
6. What mistakes do Percy, Grover, and Annabeth make when seeking entrance into the Underworld? How do they convince Charon to let them enter? *(Annabeth says they want to go to the Underworld which is the opposite of what most people say. Grover chooses an unrealistic "cause of death"—all three of them drowning in one bathtub. Percy misreads Charon's name tag, signifying he is a demigod, and does not smell dead. Percy offers golden drachmas and a promise to request a pay raise for Charon in exchange for passage across the River Styx.)*
7. What does the pollution in the River Styx represent? What examples are given in the novel? What else would you expect to see? *(The pollution consists of humans' "hopes, dreams, [and] wishes that never came true" [p. 289]. Examples include plastic dolls, crushed carnations, and soggy diplomas. Answers will vary.)*

8. Why do so many people choose the "EZ Death" line rather than risk being judged? Do you think it would be better to take the risk of being judged or know that you will spend eternity doing nothing in Asphodel Fields? *(People are afraid to be judged for their actions on Earth. Many people were not especially kind or generous during their lives; instead they merely existed, not living good or bad lives. By choosing Asphodel Fields, one avoids knowing for certain that one has lived an unremarkable life or being punished severely if one has done more harm than good throughout his/her life. Answers will vary.)*
9. Why do you think the author makes Cerberus likeable? *(Answers will vary, but students should infer that an oversized, playful dog is a reader-friendly example that reinforces one of the story's main themes, that "...everybody...need[s] a little attention once in a while" [p. 298].)*
10. **Prediction:** What will happen when Percy confronts Hades?

Supplementary Activities

1. Comprehension: Review Percy's taxi ride from Las Vegas to Santa Monica. Write an entry from the cabbie's diary giving his thoughts on the passengers and their discussions.
2. Art: Create a work of art that shows Percy receiving the pearls from the Nereid.
3. Critical Thinking: Design the "All-New Compendium of L.A. Area Monsters" (p. 282). Include telephone listings, addresses, and advertisements. You may use monsters from myths, novels, and movies or make up your own.

Chapters 19–20

The flying shoes almost drag Grover into Tartarus, the pit in Percy's dreams. Hades accuses Percy of stealing the master bolt and Hades's own powerful weapon, the helm of darkness. When Zeus's master bolt is found in Percy's backpack, Percy realizes he has been tricked. Hades produces Percy's mother, tempting Percy to save her. However, Percy chooses to continue his quest and uses the three magic pearls to escape with Annabeth and Grover. On the beach in Santa Monica, Ares admits to planting the master bolt in the backpack and shows Percy the helm of darkness, though Percy senses another powerful presence is influencing the god of war. By commanding the ocean waves, Percy defeats Ares and asks the Furies to return the helm to Hades. To return the master bolt before the deadline, Percy risks entering Zeus's domain and takes a plane to New York.

Discussion Questions

1. What does Percy mean when he looks at the crowds on the Fields of Asphodel and thinks, "The dead aren't scary. They're just sad" (p. 301). *(Answers will vary. Percy expected the dead to look scary instead of confused or angry. He sees the hopelessness of these lost souls who will spend eternity in Asphodel. Percy is coming to realize life is precious.)*
2. What can you determine from the scene at Tartarus? *(Answers will vary. The monster in the pit has limited powers. The monster controls the flying shoes and a strong, cold wind, yet momentary hesitation as Percy's sword is unsheathed seems to indicate uncertainty. The wail of outrage shows that the monster was, for some reason, very intent on possessing Annabeth, Grover, and Percy.)*

Vocabulary

obsidian
parapets
levitated
bristled
predicament
portico
fused
mesmerizing
charisma
pretense
debris
reincarnated
morphed
catapulted
recede

3. Hades is the third god Percy meets and the first one who seems godlike. Who are the other two gods? Why does Hades seem more godlike? *(Dionysus and Ares were the first two. Hades wears a crown and robes, is about ten feet tall, sits on a throne of human bones, radiates power, has a mesmerizing, evil charisma, and his aura makes Percy feel submissive. Dionysus only gave Percy a brief glimpse of his power. The god of wine wears a Hawaiian shirt, resembles someone who might play poker with Gabe, and spends most of his time playing cards and complaining about his personal circumstances. Though Ares is very intimidating, his stature is not superhuman, and he is sarcastic, has a nervousness about him, and rides around on a motorcycle in modern clothes.)*
4. What does Hades accuse Percy of doing? What do these accusations reveal about the quest? *(Hades accuses Percy of executing Poseidon's scheme to start a war, saying not only did Percy steal Zeus's master bolt but his own helm of darkness. Percy's, Annabeth's, and Grover's suspicions that there is a bigger problem than a simple theft are confirmed. They have been on the wrong track all along because someone other than Hades is manipulating Percy and pushing the gods towards war. Confronting Hades and returning Zeus's master bolt are not the end of the quest; Percy must also find the real thief and return Hades's missing helm.)*
5. Discuss Percy's choice on the best use of the three pearls. How does the prophecy affect Percy's decision? *(The prophecy is correct in that Percy will fail to save what matters most in the end—his mother. Percy puts his personal need to rescue his mother aside and accepts his duty to complete his quest. He also realizes Grover and Annabeth are not the ones who will fulfill the prophecy of betrayal by a friend.)*
6. What causes Percy to suspect Ares is not behind the plan to start a war between the gods? If Ares did not personally steal the master bolt or helm of darkness, who do you think is the thief? *(Ares twitches and briefly goes into a trance as if he is listening to another voice when Percy asks him why he did not keep the stolen master bolt. Ares accidentally reveals that he has dreams. Answers will vary.)*
7. Which of Percy's characteristics help him fight Ares? Which do you think is the most important? *(Answers will vary. Percy's temper and impetuousness prove to be a boon in this situation. His experiences with bullies taught him to taunt Ares into making the deal for the helm and bolt. Percy values friendship and listens to friends' advice, such as Annabeth's about how strength sometimes bows to wisdom, or Luke's on swordfighting. ADHD also keeps Percy alive during the battle. As the son of Poseidon, Percy has command over the ocean and cleverly uses the waves as a weapon.)*
8. Why does Mrs. Dodds's opinion of Percy change? How do you think she will treat him if they meet again? *(The Fury realizes Percy is not the thief and acknowledges him as a hero when he gives her the helm to return to Hades. Answers will vary. Though she now respects Percy, Mrs. Dodds would not hesitate to destroy him if he gave her just cause.)*
9. After something stops Ares from killing him, Percy realizes what is in the pit. In addition to his dreams, what clues are given to identify the monster? What do you think is in the pit at Tartarus? *(Light, sound, and color fade, and a pressure slows time, dropping the temperature to freezing. Life feels hopeless, and whatever made the changes is stronger than Ares and the Furies.*

Answers will vary. Observant readers will remember the story of Zeus defeating his Titan father Kronos, whose remains were thrown into Tartarus.)

10. **Prediction:** How will Zeus react when he meets Percy?

Supplementary Activities

1. Comprehension/Art: Working in teams, create dioramas of the Underworld's different areas. Combine the dioramas, and display the complete Underworld in class.
2. Math/Critical Thinking: Review Hades's complaints about the costs of ruling his kingdom. Brainstorm a list of income sources (e.g., sale of precious metals) and expenses (e.g., Charon's salary) for the Underworld. Then create an income and expense budget using a blank checkbook register to track Hades's cash flow.
3. Critical Thinking: Ares says the bloodiest kind of war is between relatives. Write an essay that explains why fighting among family members might be especially heated.
4. Science: Percy uses the tide to battle Ares. Create a visual presentation on one of the topics below:

   a) High and Low Tides—Use the following terms in your presentation: gravity, lunar phases, spring tides, and weather.

   b) The Intertidal Zone—Use the following terms in your presentation: littoral zone, habitats, ecosystem, and nutrients.

   Then describe how Poseidon would explain the scientific facts included in your presentation.

Chapters 21–22

Percy enters Mount Olympus through the Empire State Building and meets with Zeus and Poseidon. Zeus is grateful for the master bolt; however, he refuses to consider Percy's warning about Kronos healing and rising in power. Poseidon regrets Percy's birth because a hero's fate is always tragic, but he acknowledges that his son did well. Percy returns home to find his mother unscathed. However, Gabe is becoming increasingly abusive, and Poseidon has sent Percy the package containing Medusa's head. Percy debates whether he has the right to determine Gabe's fate. He comes to realize his mother has to solve her own problems and later learns that she has petrified Gabe. At Camp Half-Blood, Luke nearly kills Percy with a scorpion and admits that he serves Kronos, for whom he stole the bolt and the helm. Annabeth and Percy, both of whom choose to live with their mortal parents during the school year, agree that they will return next summer to hunt down Luke. Percy accepts the challenge of being a hero and Poseidon's son.

Discussion Questions

1. Why does Percy like the media's version of himself? What is ironic about the media's portrayal of Percy? Do you think Percy considers himself a hero? *(The media decides to depict Percy as a brave victim rather than as a juvenile delinquent. The media's illogical about-face in their portrayal of Percy happens not because they are truly convinced he is a hero but because, as Chiron noted before Percy began his quest, humans will go to incredible lengths to make events conform to their version of reality. Answers will vary.)*

Vocabulary

reality
turbulence
summit
hippodrome
banished
inverted
restrained
mimicked
tragedy
shrouds
clamoring
unanimous
solo
whaling
vengeance

2. Compare and contrast Zeus's and Hades's palaces. Why does Percy feel sorry for Hades? *(Hades built his palace to resemble Zeus's. However, Hades's palace is black and bronze instead of glittering white and silver. Answers will vary but should include that Olympus is impressive and its inhabitants are festive while the Underworld is imposing and its inhabitants are mostly depressed and angry. Percy feels sorry for Hades because the god is banished from the splendor of Olympus for most of the year.)*
3. Discuss the descriptions of Zeus and Poseidon. What can you determine about the personality of each god? *(Answers will vary. Zeus is powerful, formal, and aloof. He can be dramatic and temperamental, and he expects others to defer to him. Poseidon is sensitive, mysterious, casual, and has a sense of humor. He is practical and willing to consider others' viewpoints.)*
4. Why does Zeus refuse to discuss the possibility of Kronos healing and rising in power? What is Poseidon's opinion? *(Answers will vary. Zeus is the one who put Kronos in the pit of Tartarus. If Kronos becomes powerful again, another war between the gods and Titans could occur, and this is not something that Zeus wants to consider. Poseidon admits that Kronos is still alive, but because Kronos has always occasionally stirred, he does not believe that Kronos is on the verge of rising from the pit.)*
5. Why is Percy glad that Poseidon is so distant? How does Poseidon feel about Percy? Do you think that Percy will meet an unhappy fate? *(Percy does not consider that Poseidon protected him by not acknowledging him as a son. Instead, he believes his father does not know whether he wants him as a son, that he considers Percy a mistake, and after years of ignoring Percy, any explanations or emotions on Poseidon's part would not feel real. Poseidon does consider Percy a mistake, not because he does not want a son, but because Percy will have the unhappy fate of a hero. Poseidon recognizes his son and is proud of him. That he calls Percy's mother a queen implies Poseidon regrets not having a family life with Percy and his mother. Answers will vary. Poseidon seems sure of Percy's fate, and as a god he should have special insight into the matter. However, the Nereid described Percy's fate as "great and terrible." In addition, it is worth noting that Perseus, the hero for whom Percy is named, is the only Greek hero who does not meet an unhappy fate.)*
6. Describe Percy's struggle to decide how to deal with Gabe. How does Percy's quest affect his decision? How does Percy's quest affect his mother's decision? *(Percy knows he cannot live in a house where Gabe hits his mother and that a hero would give Gabe what he deserves; however, Percy recalls Poseidon saying a hero's story always ends in tragedy. Having seen the Underworld, Percy finds himself questioning whether he wants/has the right to determine Gabe's fate. At his mother's behest, Percy chooses to let his mother handle her own problems. Percy's mother learns from the quest that she must find the courage to take care of herself.)*
7. How has Grover changed after the quest? How do Percy and Annabeth feel about these changes? *(Grover has grown up and earned a searcher's license. He looks older and has more self-confidence. He appreciates his friendship with Percy and Annabeth but is eager to begin his life's dream of searching for Pan. Both Percy and Annabeth are worried because in 2,000 years no searcher has ever returned, yet they remain positive Grover will be the first.)*
8. How does Luke feel about the Olympians and Western civilization? What caused him to feel this way? *(Luke believes the gods have become complacent and live in the past. He feels Western civilization is harmful and not worth protecting. His solution is to start over with something more*

honest, with Kronos bringing in a new Golden Age. Luke's bitterness began after he returned from an uninspired quest to a life with no purpose, a routine life that fueled his brewing anger at the gods for Thalia's death. Kronos offers Luke the excitement of worthwhile quests with the goal of a new age, an age where the strongest will be those who serve Kronos.)

9. Percy says Annabeth's decision to go home and try again with her father "took guts." What do you think influenced Annabeth to write a letter to her father? *(Answers will vary. Annabeth respects Percy, so she followed his advice. The quest proved she can survive in the world. Also, being in the Underworld may have reminded her that a person only gets one chance at life, and not giving up on forging a bond with her family is one way she can make the most of it.)*

10. Why does Percy have trouble deciding whether to stay at Camp Half-Blood or go live with his mother? What helps him decide to go home? *(Even though hero training would be more fun than going to school, Percy wants to live with his mother, especially without Gabe. However, he is worried about whether he and his mother will survive the inevitable monster attacks. When Annabeth leaves the camp with her family, Percy feels alone. He realizes that as Poseidon's son, he cannot be restrained and determines he can survive in the world.)*

Supplementary Activities

1. Comprehension: Review the scene where Percy meets his father. Rewrite the scene from Poseidon's point of view.
2. Art/Critical Thinking: Design Grover's searcher's license. Then list the five places you think Grover will begin his search for Pan, and explain your choices.
3. Writing: Write a poem to honor Percy and his quest.
4. Literary Analysis: As a class, review the stages of the Hero's Journey. Then compare and discuss your reading journals (from Initiating Activity #5 on page 6 of this guide).

Post-reading Discussion Questions

1. What are the novel's main themes? Explain which one you think is the most important and why. *(coming of age, individuality, friendship, family, heroism, leadership, responsibility, loyalty, faith, betrayal, learning disabilities, civilization, environmental conservation; Answers will vary.)*
2. Chiron tells Percy, "...the Oracle's words often have double meanings" (p. 142). Compare and contrast what Percy expected from his prophecy with what actually happened. *("You shall go west, and face the god who has turned" [p. 141]: Percy did go west, however, the god who had turned was Ares rather than Hades; "You shall find what was stolen, and see it safely returned" [p. 141]: Percy not only found and returned Zeus's master bolt but also Hades's helm of darkness, thus preventing war between the gods; "You shall be betrayed by one who calls you a friend" [p. 141]: After worrying that Annabeth or Grover would betray him, Percy decides Ares, pretending to be his friend, fulfilled the prophecy, but the traitor is Luke; "And you shall fail to save what matters most, in the end" [p. 141]: Though Percy assumes his mother will not be released from the Underworld, Hades does return her in exchange for the helm; however, Percy does not save his mother from Gabe. Instead he does the right thing and lets her save herself.)*
3. How has Percy changed as a result of his quest? *(Answers will vary. Percy is no longer a troubled kid with low self-esteem. Through his quest he learns how to take advantage of his traits, both in battle and in life, and embrace responsibility. Percy has friends he is sure he can trust and believes in himself.)*
4. What traits make a character heroic? Provide examples of Percy's heroism. *(Answers will vary. Traits should include courage, compassion, well-defined values, confidence, and leadership abilities. Some students will say Percy makes a good hero as shown by his refusals to leave friends and family in danger, his bravery against gods and monsters, and his choice to prevent a war that would affect many rather than rescue his mother, a personal priority.)*
5. Why do half-bloods tend to have mixed emotions about their parents? Compare and contrast how Percy, Luke, and Annabeth are affected by their relationships with their parents. *(Answers will vary. Some half-bloods are especially proud of their divine parent. However, many resent one or both of their parents for ignoring them, sending them away, and/or for putting them in the difficult situation of belonging to neither the human nor the god realm. In comparing Percy, Luke, and Annabeth, it seems that the crucial difference in their development lies in whether or not and to what degree they have experienced parental love. Percy is fortunate to have a mortal mother who accepts him and all of the difficulties that come with being the mother of a demigod. She goes out of her way to protect him and give him a good life. Even her initially puzzling marriage to Smelly Gabe is revealed to be something done for Percy's safety. His loving relationship with his mother is likely the reason he is able to make a relatively smooth transition into hero life. She has given him a strong moral foundation and has always tried to make him feel valuable and important, even when the rest of the world would have him believe otherwise. After some [understandable] hesitation, confusion, and anger, Percy is able to accept his heritage, his long-estranged father, and the responsibility that comes with being a demigod. Luke, on the other hand, runs away from his human mother and seems to have a rather distant relationship with Hermes. He gives away the winged shoes that Hermes gave him, knowing full well that he will never see them again. It seems that no one has ever reached out to Luke as a parent, and he proves unable to resolve his feelings of neglect. This bitterness leaves him vulnerable to Kronos's brainwashing. Luke is so desperate for recognition and anything resembling a parent-son relationship that he welcomes Kronos's attention, even though it is negative [as evidenced by Kronos's patronizing and disparaging words to Luke in Percy's dream before his arrival in Las Vegas]. Like Luke, Annabeth is a runaway. However, unlike Luke, she has known parental love, though the rules concerning gods' relationships with godlings [only indirect influence] seem to have prevented Athena from spending much time with her. Athena*

tried to make sure that Annabeth's father would give her a good home, but Annabeth's father has, until recently, been very reluctant to forge a relationship with her. When Annabeth ran away from home, it was Athena who guided her toward help. All things considered, Annabeth is fairly well-adjusted, but she does come off as more hurt and bitter than Percy. In addition, as she has had little interaction with Athena and Athena is, until the end of the story, the only loving parent in her life [however indirectly], Annabeth is very concerned with defining herself through her connection to Athena. For example, she is always sure to say that she has a strategy because Athena would have a strategy, she will have trouble getting along with Percy because Athena had trouble getting along with Poseidon, she wants to be an architect because Athena expects her children to create things, etc. By the end of the story, with a quest behind her and some prodding from Percy, she is brave enough to make another attempt at connecting with her father.)

6. Explain how the story is a commentary on the coming-of-age process. *(Camp Half-Blood can be viewed as a metaphor for adolescence. It is a transitional place for the demigods, a place where they discover who they are and set life goals for themselves. Everyone progresses at different rates and for different reasons. Some people [like Percy and Annabeth] are ready to take on adult responsibility right away; some people [like Grover and Luke] have been stuck at one stage for a while and need someone to believe in them in order to claim their place in the world. Grover remarks that sixth grade is an especially perilous time for demigods in terms of monster attacks. This is telling because it is right around this age that many young people enter into puberty and must deal with its great physical, psychological, and emotional challenges. In light of this comment, the monster attacks then seem to represent the challenges of the maturation process. Like many mothers, Percy's mother knew all along that one day there would be things she would not be able to protect her child from, but she "selfishly" tried to keep him close to her for as long as she could. Some children, however, do not have a parent who is willing and/or able to help them through the maturation process, and Annabeth and Luke represent these children. Left to his own devices, Luke chooses the wrong path in life, but Annabeth, Grover, and Percy emerge from their quest confident in their abilities to survive in the world and make a positive impact on it. Note that shortly after successfully completing the quest, Grover appears high-school age.)*

7. In what ways are Percy's dreams important to the story? *(Answers will vary. The dreams' frightening nature builds suspense as the story progresses. Through dreams, Percy comes to understand his role as a hero caught up in a difficult and complex conflict between the gods. The dreams provide Percy, Grover, and Annabeth with key clues that eventually help them realize that their quest is not what it initially seems. Also, the dreams leave part of the story unresolved so that it can be continued in future novels [Kronos is healing and intends to rise from Tartarus.].)*

8. What messages does the author wish to send about faith? How does he use the story to illustrate faith's importance in life? *(Answers will vary. All of the heroic characters are driven by faith in one way or another. In the battle scene on the Arch, the author seems to have very deliberately put Percy in a situation where in order to have a chance at survival he must make a leap based only on the belief [however dim] that doing so will save him, i.e., literally a leap of faith. Alone on the Arch, Percy is bitten by the Chimera and has only two choices: settle for an inevitable death or take a chance and jump into the Mississippi. Echidna tells Percy, "If you are a son of Poseidon...you would not fear water.... Prove your bloodline" [p. 210]. She repeatedly ridicules Percy's lack of faith, and as the Chimera attempts to finish off Percy, Echidna calls Percy "faithless one." By praying to his father and deciding to jump, Percy shows faith in his father and in his identity as a son of Poseidon. The author seems to be telling readers that self-realization sometimes requires one to make a leap of faith and that the alternative is death [albeit usually only a figurative one, the death of the self]. Only by believing in themselves can people know and embrace their identities and fulfill their potential. However, this is sometimes difficult to do without others' support. This is especially true for Grover. Grover has been made to feel like a failure by the Council*

of Cloven Elders, but in Percy he finds someone who believes in him. Percy is unable to use the flying shoes because spending time in the air is unsafe for Poseidon's children, but with Percy's encouragement Grover becomes Percy's secret weapon, his "flying ace" who is instrumental in defeating Medusa and helping Percy and Annabeth escape from the water park. Annabeth longs for a quest because she has never really had a chance to explore the world, but she is told that she will not be allowed this chance until the arrival of "someone special." As Annabeth gets to know Percy, her faith in not only his abilities but in his character and opinions grows. When Percy advises her to again try to connect with her father, she writes her father a letter. This act gives her another chance at having a family and living in the world, but none of these positive changes could have happened until Annabeth learned to invest significant trust in someone other than herself and Athena. However, the story's best examples of faith's importance may come from Grover, Annabeth, and Percy's trip to the Underworld. The River Styx is littered with plastic dolls, crushed carnations, and soggy diplomas, symbols of "hopes, dreams, [and] wishes that never came true" [p. 289]. By describing the path to death as littered with abandoned hopes, the author reminds readers that a life without faith is purposeless and equivalent to/leads to death. However horrible receiving eternal punishment in the Underworld may be, in some ways the people in Asphodel Fields seem more tragic. By not making their own leaps of faith in life and/or in death [by choosing the EZ Death option], they are doomed to a completely unremarkable eternity. The author does not want people to waste their lives by living faithlessly and always choosing the "safe" option.)

9. Why do you think the author made Percy a character with dyslexia and ADHD? Why is this detail important to the story's message? *(Answers will vary, but Riordan says he gave Percy the same learning disabilities as his son to show that being different is not a bad thing, that it can actually be a sign of talent. In interviews, the author states that he wrote* The Lightning Thief *to interest kids in Greek mythology and to honor kids with learning disabilities. One of the story's main themes is that "everybody...need[s] a little attention once in a while" [p. 298]. Because of his disabilities, Percy often feels that he cannot do anything right. By working with a main character who has struggled through life and has a fractured ego, the writer is able to show how positive attention can buoy someone's spirit, make him/her believe in him/herself, and motivate him/her to achieve great things.)*

10. What about *The Lightning Thief* did you like best? What did you like least? Would you read the next novel in the series? Why or why not? *(Answers will vary.)*

Post-reading Extension Activities

Writing

1. Write a story about Percy visiting Poseidon's kingdom under the sea. Your story should have a beginning, middle, and end.
2. Create a race of monsters to replace the role filled by the Furies in the novel. Write a letter to Hades. Convince the god of the Underworld that your monsters are superior to the Furies.
3. Write an original myth about how something in your state came to be. Use the stages of the Hero's Journey to outline your myth.
4. Imagine you are the Oracle. Write a prophecy that describes an upcoming school field trip or event. Word your prophecy mysteriously so that it contains hidden or double meanings.

Art

5. In the novel, Ares is portrayed as a biker and Zeus wears a pinstriped suit. Create a collage showing other Greek gods and creatures as you think they would appear in the modern world.
6. Invent your own god or demigod. Create artwork that shows your character's appearance, specific job, special powers, symbols, and weapons.
7. Research Greek vases. Design a vase that illustrates a myth from one of the following topics: a) plant and flower myths (e.g., Persephone and pomegranate seeds) or b) constellation myths (e.g., Centaurus).
8. Review the predictions you made while reading the novel. Choose one of your incorrect predictions. Create artwork that shows how the novel would have changed if your prediction had come true.

Social Studies

9. Read two versions of the same Greek myth. Use a Venn diagram to record any differences in details.
10. Prepare a time line showing the probable locations of Mount Olympus as the heart of Western civilization. Include visual displays and brief reports about each location.
11. Research the history of the Olympics. Then organize a mock Olympics competition with your class.

Listening/Speaking

12. Write a humorous short story about Chiron training a hero in the year 2200. Then read your story aloud in class.
13. View the film *Percy Jackson & The Olympians: The Lightning Thief*, and discuss similarities between the film and the novel with your classmates.

Drama

14. Working with a small group, write and stage a scene from the novel. Add appropriate background music and lighting.
15. Create a video of one myth from your illustrated encyclopedia (Supplementary Activity #3 on page 8 of this guide). Include costumes, settings, and background music.

Assessment for *The Lightning Thief*

Assessment is an ongoing process. The following ten items can be completed during study of the novel. Once finished, the student and teacher will check the work. Points may be added to indicate the level of understanding.

Name ______________________________ Date ______________

Student	Teacher	
_______	_______	1. Complete the Story Map on page 35 of this guide.
_______	_______	2. Choose what you feel is the best example of the novel's use of humor. It can be a sentence, paragraph, or scene. Write a paragraph explaining your choice.
_______	_______	3. Complete the Cause and Effect chart on page 36 of this guide.
_______	_______	4. Complete the Feelings chart on page 37 of this guide. On a separate sheet of paper, write a paragraph that explains what Percy discovers about himself during his quest.
_______	_______	5. Complete at least two Post-reading Extension Activities, and present one to the class.
_______	_______	6. Write a review that compares *The Lightning Thief* to another fantasy story. In your essay, use information from both works to support your ideas.
_______	_______	7. Write an essay on what you have learned about Greek mythology from reading *The Lightning Thief*. Include your thoughts about viewing mythological creatures in a modern setting.
_______	_______	8. Correct all quizzes taken over the novel.
_______	_______	9. In an essay, identify one theme in the novel and explain the part it plays in the story and in the author's message to readers.
_______	_______	10. Using at least ten vocabulary words, write a summary of the novel.

Prediction Chart

What characters have we met so far?	What is the conflict in the story?	What are your predictions?	Why did you make these predictions?

Target Word Chart

Directions: Complete the chart below for your chosen word.

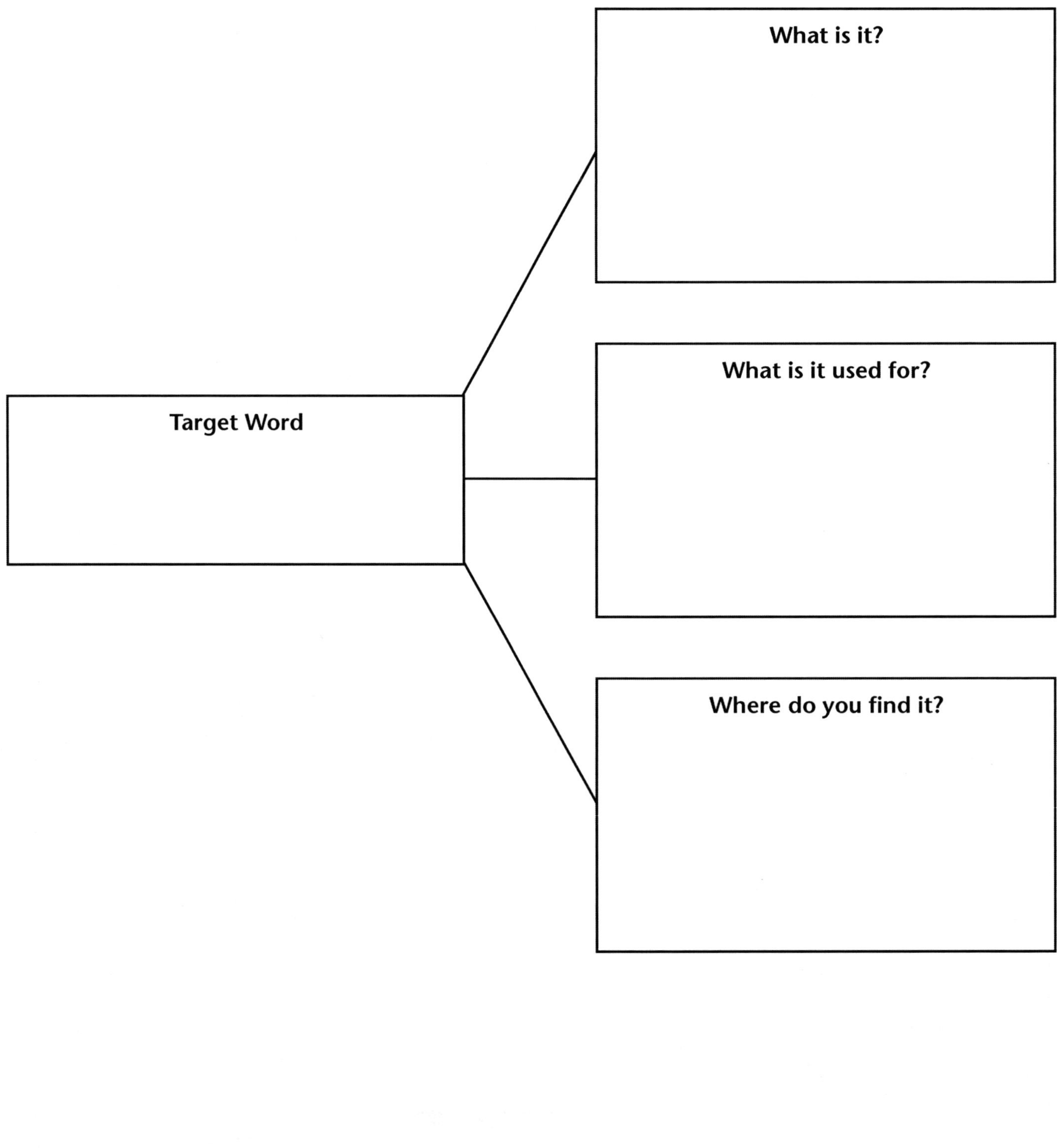

Character Web

Directions: Choose a character from the novel and complete the chart below. Cite evidence from the story as you fill in information.

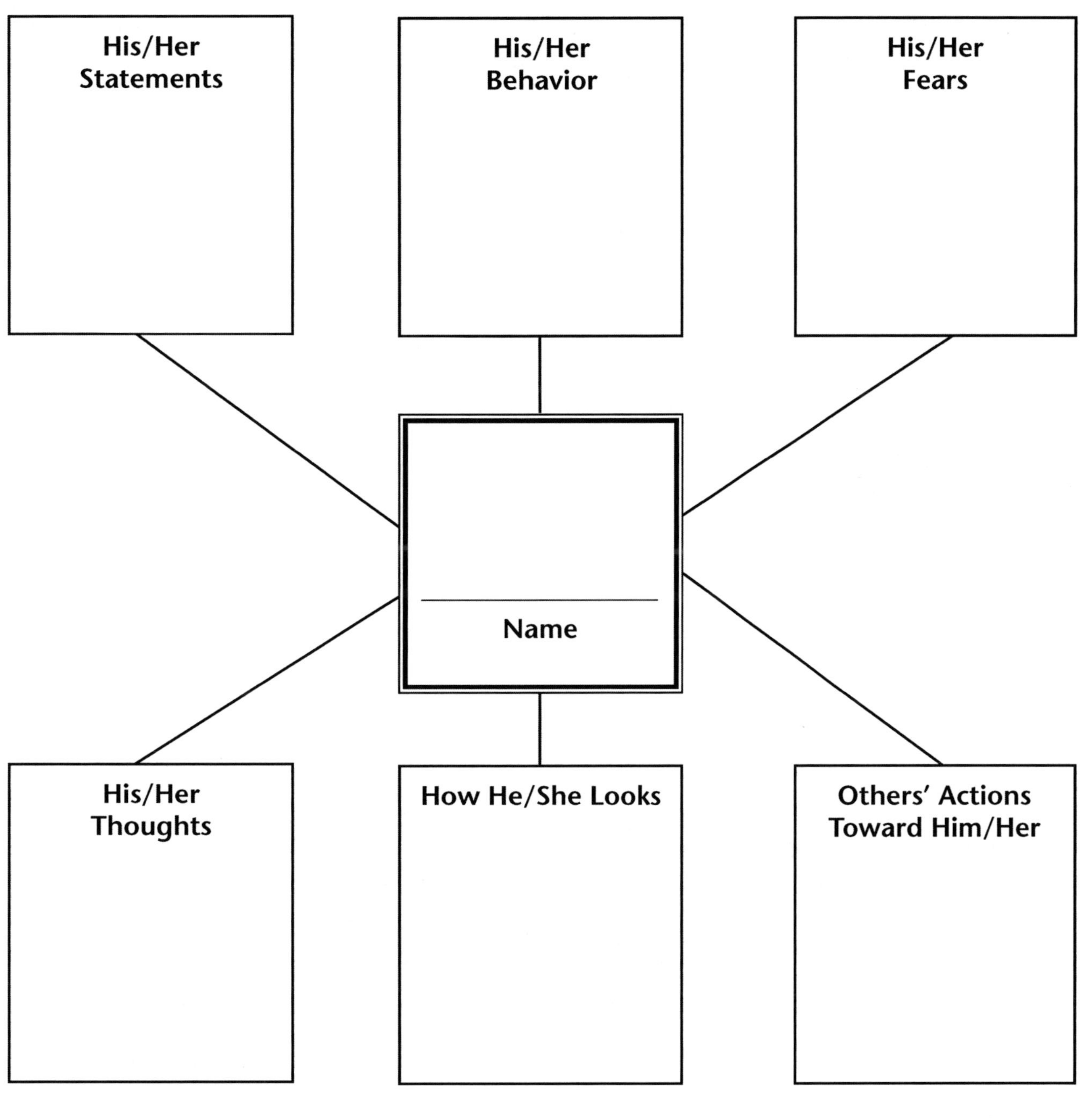

Flock Together

Directions: Explain on one feather how Percy Jackson is similar to his namesake Perseus. On the other, explain how the characters are different from each other. Use reference materials when necessary.

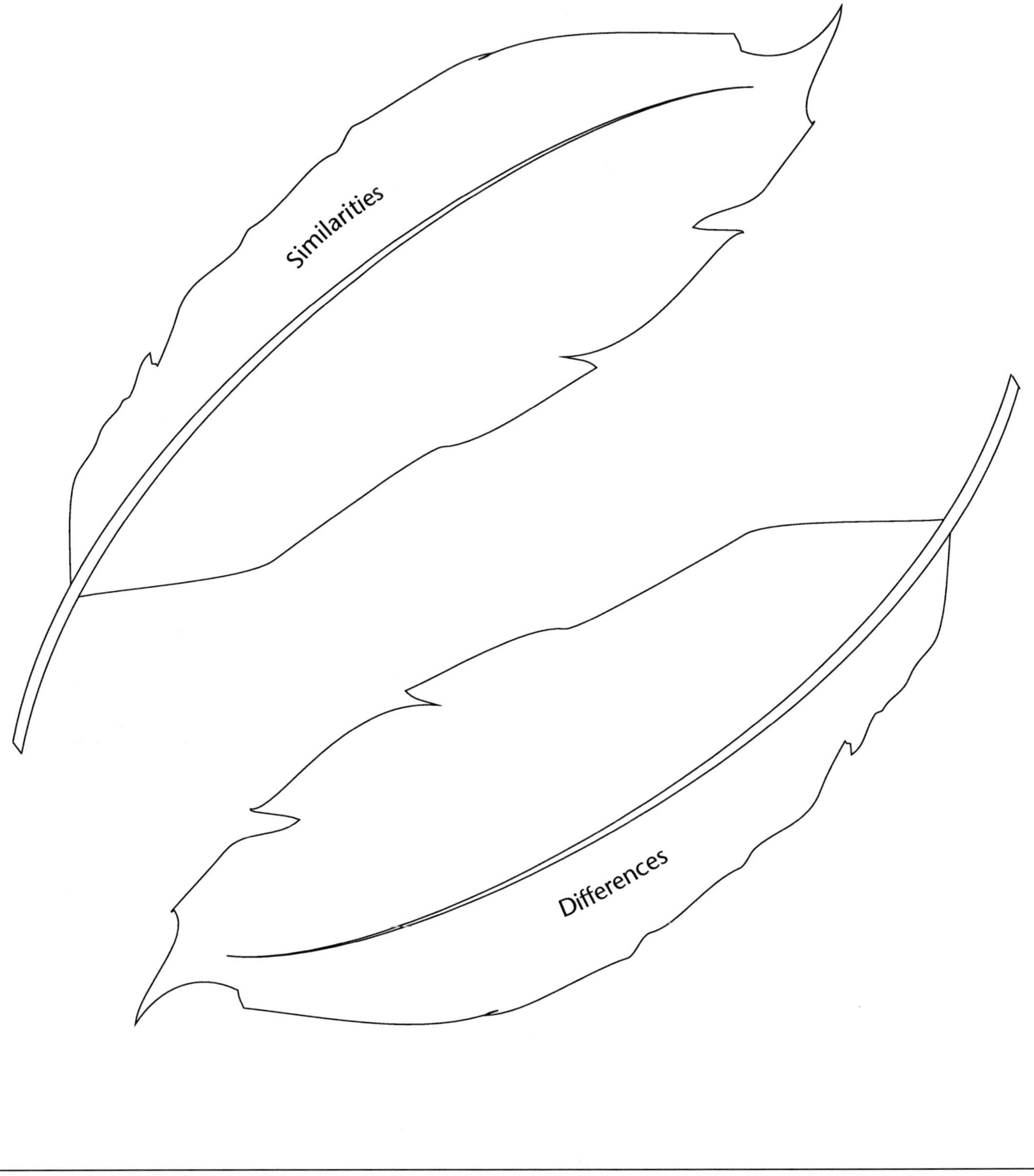

Story Map

Directions: Complete the story map for *The Lightning Thief.*

Characters____

____

Time and Place____________________________________

____

Problem____

____

____

Goal____

____

____

Beginning ⟶ Development ⟶ Outcome

____

____

____

____

Resolution____

____

____

____

Cause and Effect

Directions: Write four events from the story, and then list the effect of each event.

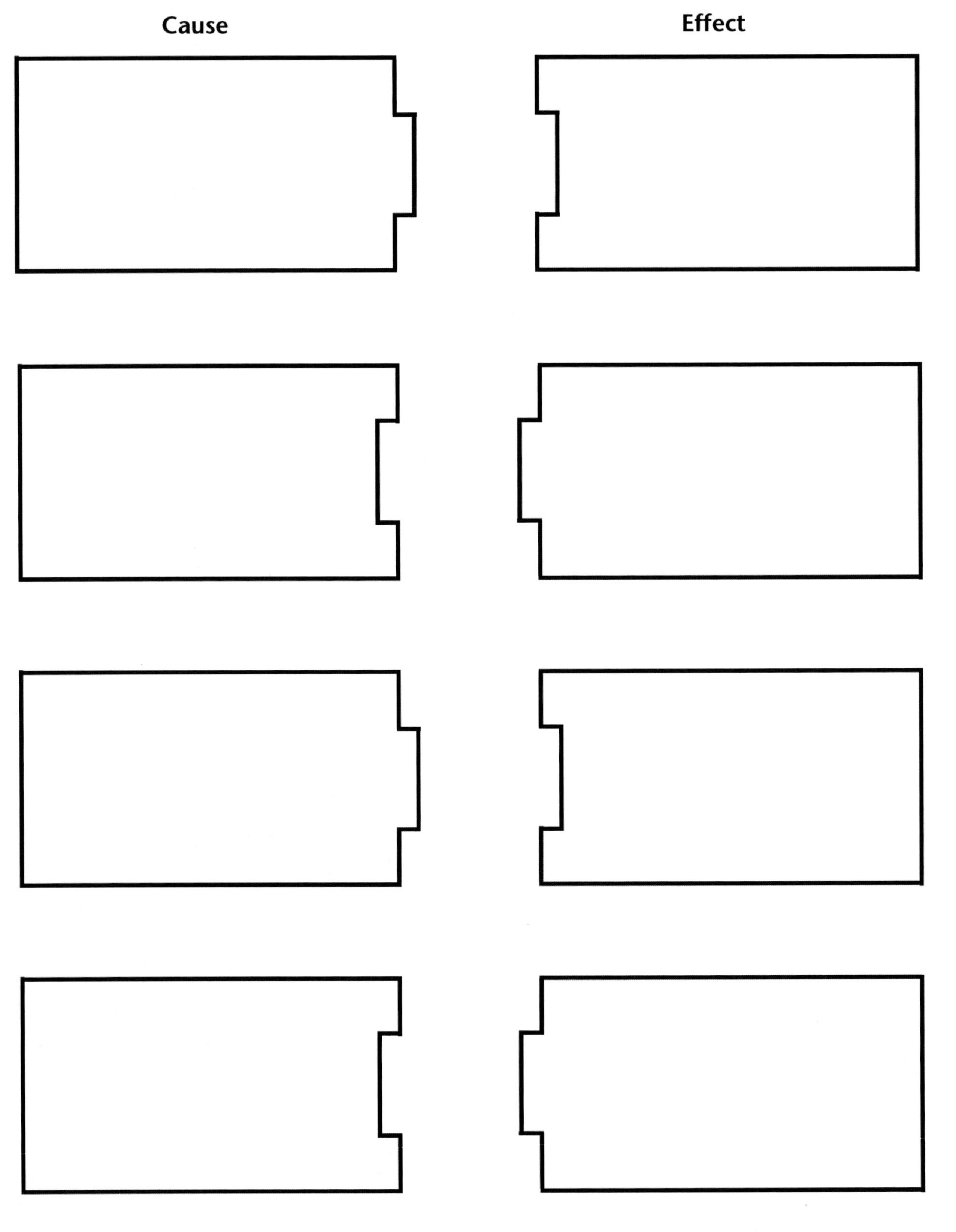

Feelings

Directions: Complete the chart below for Percy.

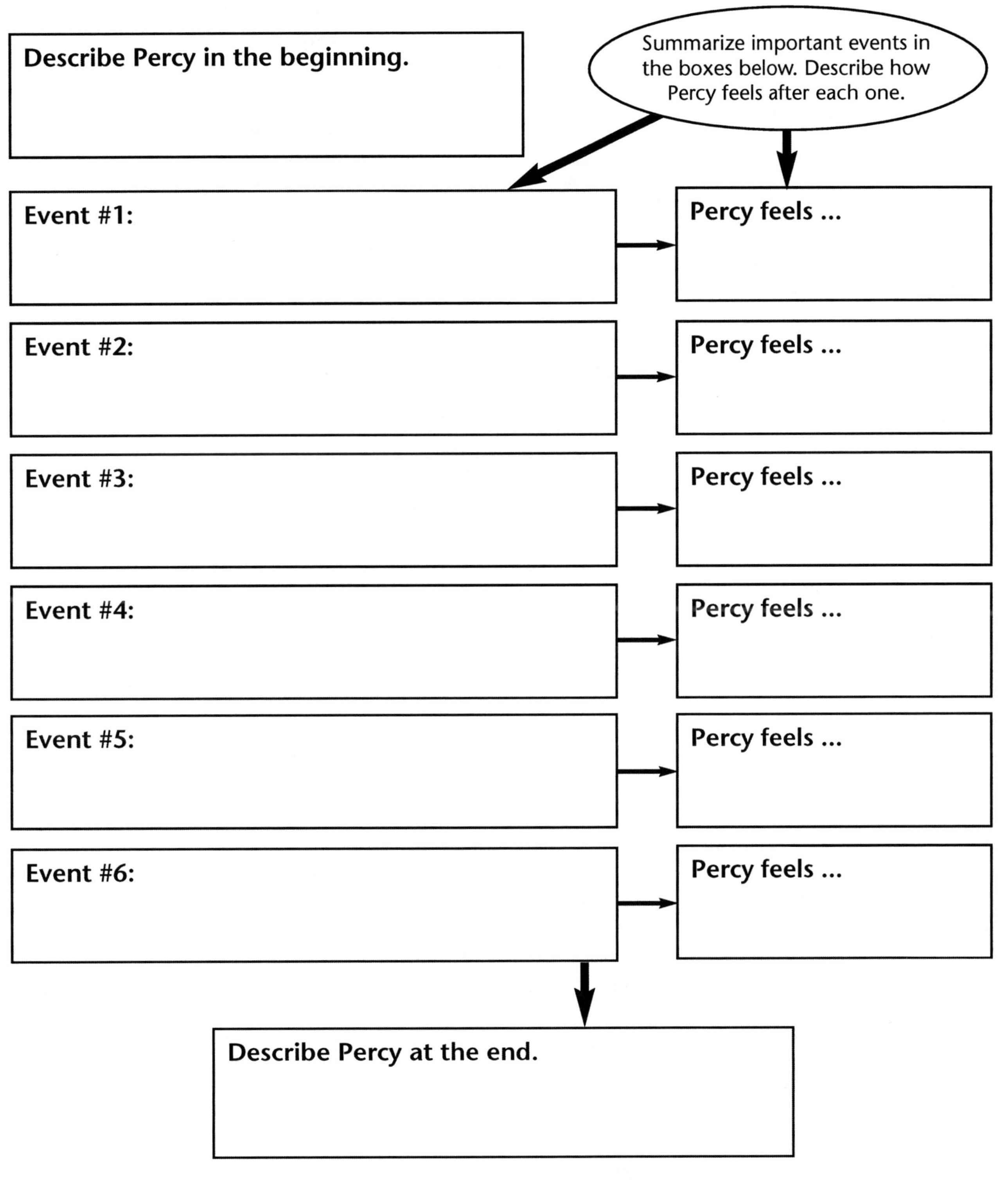

Linking Novel Units® Lessons to National and State Reading Assessments

During the past several years, an increasing number of students have faced some form of state-mandated competency testing in reading. Many states now administer state-developed assessments to measure the skills and knowledge emphasized in their particular reading curriculum. The discussion questions and post-reading questions in this Novel Units® Teacher Guide make excellent open-ended comprehension questions and may be used throughout the daily lessons as practice activities. The rubric below provides important information for evaluating responses to open-ended comprehension questions. Teachers may also use scoring rubrics provided for their own state's competency test.

Please note: The Novel Units® Student Packet contains optional open-ended questions in a format similar to many national and state reading assessments.

Scoring Rubric for Open-Ended Items

3-Exemplary	Thorough, complete ideas/information Clear organization throughout Logical reasoning/conclusions Thorough understanding of reading task Accurate, complete response
2-Sufficient	Many relevant ideas/pieces of information Clear organization throughout most of response Minor problems in logical reasoning/conclusions General understanding of reading task Generally accurate and complete response
1-Partially Sufficient	Minimally relevant ideas/information Obvious gaps in organization Obvious problems in logical reasoning/conclusions Minimal understanding of reading task Inaccuracies/incomplete response
0-Insufficient	Irrelevant ideas/information No coherent organization Major problems in logical reasoning/conclusions Little or no understanding of reading task Generally inaccurate/incomplete response

Notes

Notes

